Fly With Eagles

Fly With Eagles

✦

Reclaiming Your Spiritual Self

Segue Baah

iUniverse, Inc.

New York Lincoln Shanghai

Fly With Eagles
Reclaiming Your Spiritual Self

iUniverse books may be ordered through booksellers or by contacting:

iUniverse
2021 Pine Lake Road, Suite 100
Lincoln, NE 68512
www.iuniverse.com
1-800-Authors (1-800-288-4677)

ISBN-13: 978-0-595-40114-7 (pbk)
ISBN-13: 978-0-595-84495-1 (ebk)
ISBN-10: 0-595-40114-7 (pbk)
ISBN-10: 0-595-84495-2 (ebk)

Printed in the United States of America

This is dedicated to Great Spirit, my Ancestors, Wind Spirit Guide, Eagle Spirit, and all Masters, Guides, Helpers, Totems, and Elementals who helped me through this effort and throughout my life.

Contents

Preface ix

Acknowledgments xi

Prayer of Invocation xiii

Time to Become Who You Really Are 1

Look to the Heavens 5

Own Your Potential 8

Prepare 11

Breathe Life 13

Choose Growth 16

Discover the Power Within 19

Accept Guidance 22

Reclaim Your Spiritual Powers 24

Notice Symbols 27

Study Mirrors 30

Face Your Fear 32

Sculpt Your Own Image 34

Transmute the Negative 36

Appreciate the Vastness 38

Expand Your Boundaries 40

Awaken to the Spiritual 42

Be of One Mind 45

Live a Prayer 46

Honor Spiritual Law 48

Accept Your Blessings 49

Be Alive 51

Open to Possibility 53

Choose Your Dream 55

Proceed in Grace 57

Celebrate 59

Let Yourself Soar 61

Prayer of Release and Surrender 63

Preface

For too long, we women have swallowed dignity, intelligence, beauty, and individuality; we have hidden away our sexual needs and desires; we have hidden inside our dreams and our very lives, for the sake of men and the society they rule. We have surrendered ourselves to the dictates of others and have enabled our enslavement with the silence that followed. We have cowered in the shadows, unable to speak or defend ourselves, our children, or our dreams. We have sat so long in silence that we can no longer remember who we are: intuitive knowers and communicators; compassionate peacemakers, dream makers, and creators of a new paradigm; world-bridgers and healers; spiritual beings, telepathic beings; sensuous, sexual, powerful—women.

Violence and injustice rage everywhere—on the streets, in marriages, among our schoolchildren, and beneath the fallout of enemy strikes in warfare. We wonder what has happened to our country and when all the violence will end. This is the fruit of the seeds we have sown. This is the harvest of our neglect and quiescence, the devouring of our feminine powers and knowing. Our collective silence has enabled violence to escalate in our homes, our cities, our nations—and our minds. We have allowed the weak, the despotic, the incompetent, and the egotistical to rule and to dominate our lives.

But now we are awakening. We are called to remember our feminine powers. Indeed, we are called to rekindle those inherent abilities through which we can reclaim our lives, children and relationships, our nation, and our world. We are called back to our spiritual selves.

For me, as a Native American woman, life has always been about spiritual awareness. In times of crisis, I choose to center on appreciation. The inner balance I've learned to rely on allows me to feel compassion for those who grieve, without getting caught up in the frenzy of seeking revenge. I see every event as a mirror held up for me to better see and understand myself.

Perhaps you, dear reader, may have reached for this book because your background is devoid of tradition. Perhaps it lacks meaning. No matter the reason, what is important is this: Life is rich with possibility. You can consciously choose to change. You can purposely decide to work on your individual shortcomings and give voice to your desires.

The following twenty-eight chapters are designed to guide you in reawakening your true self. You may want to read one for every day of a single moon cycle—the menstrual cycle of your body. Or you may want to concentrate on the particular ones you find helpful. You may even wish to work on one area or passage and meditate on it for a whole month. As you take each message to heart, watch your new life unfold as you consciously pay attention to what is happening—or not happening—in your life.

It is important to realize that your dreams need not come at the expense of others. You need not fear that there is not enough or that you will not get what you need or desire, for fear is the enemy of love, imagination, and creativity. Fear is the force that enables the bullies and abusers to have tyrannical control over our lives, children, homes, and nation.

Courage means facing your individual fears and, despite those fears, pursuing what you know deep within yourself to be right and true. Once you face your own fears and proceed in spite of them, you become a free person. As you progress, each subsequent undertaking becomes less fearsome. Each effort enables you to become more self-empowered. It is then that the embers of love, imagination, and creativity begin to stir. With every endeavor of self-expression, you will awaken to a greater understanding of your True Woman Self. Your very life will become a song to God.

Acknowledgments

I wish to thank and acknowledge Louise Mita, Pamela Graham, Sybil Vaughn, Maureen Alyea, Maynard and Jackie Eakan, Audrey Sunnyboy, Barbara Flaherty, Eileen Monaghan, Diana D. Light, Albert and Rose Damon, and Dorinda Caurisma for their love, prayer, and support. Thank you for being there for me and for your encouragement and readings.

I also thank and acknowledge LuAnne Dowling, my first editor, who encouraged me to use my Native American name. Together we added "Segue" to the name Baah ("woman"), given to me by Albert Damon, the medicine man with whom I pray. As we shared names, I called her "Heyoka," and she offered "Segue," as this is a book about transitions and women.

Finally, I thank and acknowledge Dawn Brunke, my second editor. She helped guide me through the maze of my thoughts, grounded me to the planet, and graced me with clarity.

Prayer of Invocation

Mother-Father God, we call out to you in our time of darkness, need, suffering, depression, fear, and confusion. Bless us to find our way through the maze of our lives and to see you in the darkness. Bless us to find our true feminine selves and, in finding ourselves, to find you and your true image and likeness within ourselves. Bless us to be open and honest, to be truthful and conscious, and to be accepting of ourselves as we are in darkness and light, in our fearfulness and our beauty. Bless us to be all that you created us to be.

Spirit Most High, we give thanks for all that you have blessed us to have and to be. We welcome all that our futures offer, and we totally release our past. Thank you for our past and for our present. Thank you for the blessings that are our future. May we come to know you and serve you in deeper intimacy, and at the level that will give you all the glory and honor. May we be all that you created us to be here on the Earth plane in glory, in awesome magnificence, and in total joy and happiness. May we bring your glory and awesome presence to the Earth plane in your great and wondrous way. And so it is.

Time to Become Who You Really Are

Nulato, Alaska, is a village of three hundred people. It is 350 miles away from any city and less than two degrees south of the Arctic Circle. Throughout my child hood in Nulato, I knew all of my Athabascan relatives to be very family- and village-oriented. They had little or no interest in the Western world. Although we never discussed it, I developed a strong impression that the roles for western women were confined to a grinding stereotype of housewife or slave. I thought that the role ate up young girls and women and spat them out later. It was clear to me that the role was not for me, for how could I function or grow into any greatness of being? I wanted to be free and have fun; I wanted to live!

I later took up residence in the Western world. Not wanting to be caught in the housewife/slave mess, I struggled to beat men at their own games. I focused all of my attention and energies on outdistancing them and evading society's demands. But in so doing, I became entrenched in the stereotypical ruts that were stuck in my mind, not realizing that they had been created by a male-dominant society. I was caught in their groove and enslaved by my job. What I thought was freedom in my choice of jobs began to look strange and unattractive to me as I began to realize that I wasn't really doing what I wanted to be doing. I didn't want to be a housewife, but I was still a slave to an eight-to-five job. I may not have matched the usual stereotypical roles, but I was nonetheless controlled in my daily routine.

The only way for me to escape was to stop and face what I was running from. I could change bad habits or negative choices only by looking at them, recognizing their patterns, and consciously choosing new behaviors. To release old patterns and develop a plan for my life on my own terms, I turned my focus on me: *Who am I? What do I want? Do I want it because I really want it, or because society says it's desirable?* I found myself choosing to do things because I enjoyed doing them, even if I did them alone. I did not need a public escort, and I did not care what anyone thought of my choices.

1

To make these changes, I called on my spiritual guides. They have always been consciously present to me, and they have helped me to make many wise choices in life. These guides are what some might call angels, intuition, inner feelings, or a sense of knowing. Others may call them "the still, small voice within." However you might know them or whatever you might call them, to me, they are my guides. You can meet your guides in your dreams, meditations, deep thoughts, and prayers. Once you become aware of their presence, ask them their names. They will let you know, and they will respond to your questions and requests for guidance or clarification.

My guides were relentless in leading me to realize my spiritual strength and stamina. They taught me to pace myself—to not exhaust or fatigue my physical or mental being—as they helped me to develop my potential. "It does not matter when you arrive or how you arrive," they said. "It only matters that you take care not to get burned out in the process." My guides cautioned me against taking on more than I could handle.

With spiritual guidance, I learned to respect, honor, and seek other women of power. I came to realize how important it is to associate with these powerful women. We all need to share our lessons and learn from one another. We also empower ourselves when we enhance the growth and spiritual development of others around us.

My guides warned me about the dangers of stress, self-denial, and self-neglect. They urged me to love and care for my own well-being as I care for those I love. I was advised to seek happiness, self-fulfillment, and self-actualization, and to be appreciative of all that I had accomplished. My task, my guides told me, is to create greater spiritual awareness and power in myself. In that way, I can also help other people transform their physical and mental beings through spiritual development. Real change can happen in the world when each one of us assumes self-responsibility in this way.

We are not here to destroy or negate our physical bodies and mental abilities, but to balance and increase their potential through the infusion of Spirit. If we are indeed created in the image and likeness of God, then it is time for each one of us to begin to live up to that promise. It is time to acknowledge, accept, and receive all of our spiritual gifts, powers, abilities, and knowing. It is time to assume responsibility for our own individual spiritual growth and development. Women must take action now!

Yes, it is time for you to become who you are. You have been preparing for this time all of your life and for all the lifetimes that you have had. It is now time for the real you to stand up, be recognized, and stride awesomely onto the Earth plane.

We begin to find balance within our souls when we truly pay attention. With personal integrity guiding us, we can stop feeling so alone and begin to stand in our own truth. We become balanced by being mindful of our opinions, speaking our truth, and staying balanced in the now.

Yet it is also essential to explore our shadow side until we discover the supernatural and sacred within. We can do this by slowing down and taking time to reflect on who we are. We can do this by daring to look within our feelings—especially those feelings that we may consider negative or dark. These might include feelings of hate, rage, strong dislike, or resentment. When we look at what we don't like about ourselves, we are exploring our shadow side.

Negative feelings or thoughts may lead us to core fears and uncertainties that we can learn to face and change. This "shadow material" may lead us to a clearer vision of who we really are, to discover why we feel this way or think of someone in that manner. Once we accept and allow ourselves to feel and acknowledge these inner feelings and thoughts, we can change them.

As we uncover more of our inner shadow, we begin to discover more of the supernatural and sacred within ourselves. We begin to see how wonderful and godlike we are, how powerful we are in our own lives. We become more spiritually focused in our choices, and as we do, we become more godlike. As this god-self begins to freely emerge, we more easily recognize the sacredness of all life. We accept that we too are sacred, and we begin to make choices accordingly.

Then we end our fear of speaking the truth; indeed, we release a truth-speaking genie from within ourselves. We take the best of all of our lives and lessons, release the negatives to Mother Earth, and fly into our futures. We create a world of love, kindness, harmony, and peace. We accept change with grace and dignity. We release old habits and fears and let go of negative memories and beliefs. We also permit ourselves to begin anew and receive the abundance that we so richly deserve. We learn to accept the happiness, love, friendship, fun, joy, and exuberance of life.

In doing so, we let the universe see and hear this explosion! We let it know the expression of our lives. We let all glory and praise be released. We ride the breeze of Great Spirit to our fullness and enjoy every moment of it. We have earned our wings, and now is the time for us to soar and implement all of our magnificent gifts and powers. It is time. It is time.

First Steps

As you begin on your journey, you may wish to know your spirit guides. To do this, enter into a quiet time of meditation, prayer, or inner reflection. Breathe deeply to settle and quiet yourself. As you feel at peace, invite your guides to join you and reveal themselves to you.

Be open to whomever or whatever comes. Your guide might manifest as a bird; a man, woman, or child; an angel; an animal; a being; or a sound. Once you notice who or what has come to you, ask its name and ask to establish a clear form of communication. It could be mental communication as telepathy or shared thoughts. It could be a shared sense of feeling or a visual image for you to discern the meaning of. It could be a feeling in your body or guidance to explore books, movies, songs, CDs, etc.

Having established contact, it is now up to you to call on your guides and learn about them. Perhaps you will want to study how they relate to you and to the events and issues in your life. Your guides may also visit you in dreams, meditations, prayers, and insights or inspired thoughts.

Look to the Heavens

All of nature speaks to you about your circumstances. If you don't understand the language of symbols, however, you may encounter difficulty in making sense of your life.

Nature helps us to better see ourselves in many ways. For example, every twenty-eight years, people experience a "Saturn return." In astrological terms, a Saturn return ushers in a period of reflection on what is happening or not happening in your life. At around age twenty-seven or twenty-eight (and again at ages fifty-six and eighty-four), each individual will experience a period of time in which he or she will make a choice to continue the status quo or to do something radically different.

If a Saturn return review shows a life that is in the dumps, people tend to leave by accidents, suicides, or other means, including illness. If the reflections are positive visions of the future with promises of improvement, people tend to stay and have hope for their future. But what if an individual with a negative review simply didn't understand the symbols and images of his or her life? What if that darkness was only a very loud warning to change some negative behaviors or some aspect of life?

If we are to assess our lives at given astrological years, we would be wise to learn something about the symbols of our lives—especially if those symbols suggest a change.

Astrology isn't a locked-in destiny. Rather, it's another opportunity to do something about your current situation. In the same manner, prophecy isn't necessarily a way to spread doom and gloom. If the prophetic images are of destruction and darkness, then the recipients of such negative tidings are free to pray for change and work to manifest those changes in their lives.

We are all able to manifest change in our behaviors and actions every day. But if we aren't paying attention, we may lean toward suicide, illness, or anything that will get us out of a life that seems too dull and dark. However, we needn't go to such extremes, and it isn't all that difficult to work out. If you figure out the plot of a movie before the scenes unfold, you can figure out the images, symbols, and messages of your own life in the same way. It only takes conscious effort.

5

How to begin? Be deliberately aware of what you do, say, think, feel, hear, smell, intuit, and know. What is your sense of what is happening? What is your hunch? What is your feeling? What do you see? Pay attention and seek the messages life offers to you in every event and person.

Dare to create joy, wonder, and excitement in your life by learning what your body, life, and environment are revealing to you. Look for the meanings, messages, and miracles that the universe offers you on a daily basis.

As a very small child playing and sliding down a riverbank, I became aware of an ice crystal on a willow. As I stopped and gazed upon its beauty and rainbow colors, I felt such appreciation and awe that I was suddenly aware of God in all that was beautiful. As I focused on that god-beauty, I was transported out of my body and embraced by Mother God. I looked down and saw myself standing there, gazing at the ice crystal. In that moment of my recognition of God in nature, the beauty of it all reached out and touched my soul, leaving me unaware of my own existence, yet totally in oneness with the universe, God, Nature, and all that was love, beauty, wisdom, and grace.

You too can do this, by creating celebration in even small ways. Stop, pay attention, smile, and laugh; join friends and share your happiness over a cup of tea or coffee. Let your life and nature speak to you. Enjoy and share the beauty of simple things: the sunset or sunrise, the mountains, the dew on the grass. Call a friend and tell her about something you just figured out for yourself. *I just fixed the vacuum cleaner that has been jammed for days! I had an "aha" moment over something that has been bothering me!* Weave your own images and symbols into the creation of a wondrous life—a festival of all that you are in beauty, grace, dance, song, and laughter.

You have a wonderful occasion to begin this new process every month. In each of your moon cycles (your menstrual cycle), you have the opportunity to ponder, review, and reflect. In fact, your personal moon cycle is a particularly magnificent time for you to seed, seek, and see the changes you wish to make. Be sure to take some quiet time for yourself to meditate and reflect. You deserve it!

The importance of looking to the heavens—whether by using astrology or paying attention to the details and people in your life—is that it allows you to recognize the bounty that life presents. By paying attention, you begin to recognize and interpret the symbols and clues that life offers you. Once you begin to consciously live your life, the quality of life itself improves.

An Exercise in Colorful Attention

We begin to recognize the symbols and clues of our lives simply by paying attention. One way to begin paying attention is to keep a journal or write down your self-observations and review them from time to time, until you are familiar with them. For example, you might notice the colors you were wearing on particular day and the feelings you experienced. With these simple clues, you can begin to figure out what your feelings mean (and look like) to you.

One very old system that makes use of color and feelings is the chakra system. Chakras are energy centers of the body, each of which is associated with a particular feeling and color. The first chakra is at the base of your spine. Its color is red, and it addresses issues of fear, flight, and survival. The second chakra, found in the navel area, is orange and deals with creativity and sexuality. The third chakra is your solar plexus (found around the center of your upper abdomen) and is yellow in color. It deals with power and will. The fourth chakra is the heart. It is green and it naturally deals with issues of the heart. The fifth chakra is your throat chakra. Its color is blue and it deals with voice and your ability to speak your truth. The sixth chakra is also called the "Third Eye," for it rests between your eyebrows. This chakra is indigo in color and deals with spirituality. The seventh is the crown chakra. It sits, like a crown, on top of your head, and is white or violet in color. This chakra deals with Source and Creation issues.

I taught myself more about colors through journaling and self-observation and by asking my guides for assistance. I began to discern what colors and different body sensations meant to me, and through that, what my life and circumstances were revealing to me.

For instance, if you are dreaming about the base of your spine or about the color red, you may be dealing with base chakra energy. If you notice this, you might ask yourself whether your dream reveals some issues of fear, flight, or survival (all base chakra "feelings"). Are these issues present in your daily life, or in memories that you are addressing? If so, you might ask, "Am I afraid of something or someone? Do I feel like running away or bolting? Am I afraid that I don't have enough love, money, friends, support, or food?" Take time to ponder your answers, recording both your questions and insights in a journal. Do your words answer or resolve questions you've had or the things you've wondered about? As you proceed, be sure to allow your body and guides to help you discern what is true for you and what is not.

Own Your Potential

As each woman changes her individual reality, together we can recreate the reality of the Earth. When we each practice self-responsibility, we create specific changes in our lives and environment. Taking responsibility for ourselves empowers us and inspires us as to what we need to do or address next.

How might we start doing this? Begin by honoring the past as a teacher. This allows us to learn the lessons of our lives and lessons from our mistakes. Self-responsibility enables us to see and accept our present as our own creation. We can then live our future as an inspired dream, because we have done all that we can to live that dream, to dream that dream, and to manifest it as our reality. It is all a process, and we can control that process.

In comparison, suppression and denial of emotions stymies our growth. Why? Because we are refusing to be self-responsible. When we suppress or deny our emotions, we refuse to accept our part in life. We refuse to acknowledge the lessons provided to us. Our emotions enable us to see, feel, and experience what is and isn't working for us; emotions show us what needs to be changed.

Releasing old habits and projections of your own self-image on others allows you to be self-responsible. In this way, you can remake yourself and become the awesome, magnificent, wondrous, beautiful person you were created to be. You can become that person right here—right now!

Stay open to your inner truth as it is being revealed to you in your dreams, meditations, prayers, and inner reflections. Remain conscious of your choices as you move into your new sense of reality with confidence. In other words, don't just dream of being loved and loving—become the love and loving. *Be* it. You can and do know the unknowable.

You can become a master of illusion, for all of life is an illusion. Reality is the illusion that you currently see and the drama you are involved in at this time. So dare to ask yourself: What am I feeling? What do I need? What is the outcome that I desire?

You limit yourself by seeing only your own habitual perceptions and by relying solely on your left brain, without the integration and influence of the intuition and spiritual knowing of your right brain. So spend time becoming familiar with the gifts of both sides of your brain. The intuition, spiritual knowing, insights, creative imagination, and expressions of your right brain bring vastness to what your left brain offers. As you become more familiar with your right brain, enjoy, play, and be creative and free with your expressions and creations.

An Introduction to Right-Brain Creativity

Want a quick, simple way to access your right-brain creativity? Find a quiet, comfortable space in which to settle yourself. Begin with three deep breaths to really settle in, and then resume normal breathing.

Now close your eyes and allow yourself to visit a place you have not seen before. Take your time as you fully appreciate the scene and experience the sights, sounds, and smells, just as if you were sitting in or walking into the picture.

As you come out of your experience, take some time to describe it—either to a friend or in your journal. By recording your images, you begin to trust what you see, sense, feel, and know. Note down all the descriptive details you can recall. In this way, you not only open up to the creative wonder of the right brain, but you begin to build a bridge between left-brain and right-brain activity.

You can also enter Higher Realms and other dimensions through prayer, meditation, and conscious (or lucid) dreaming. As I began to enter other dimensions, I first paid attention to see which of my guides were present. I intuitively switched to telepathic communication and a heightened state of awareness, because I had already established with my guides that this is how they like to communicate with me. Telepathic communication is much quicker and easier for me, as when I am in other dimensions, things happen much faster.

In my meditations, I was calm yet open and accepting of what was being presented on all levels—mentally, psychologically, physically, and emotionally. I also paid attention to my alternatives and choices. What did my feelings, senses, and discernment tell me? I proceeded, knowing that my guides would lead me, observe me, and watch over me. I knew that I would safely return to the Earth plane once I garnered the messages, clues, symbols, and lessons of the meditation, prayer, dream, or inner seeking.

As you look within and come to know yourself spiritually, you will also begin to recognize the symbols and clues of you inner world. In this way, you begin to own your potential. You begin to recognize and feel that you can do anything that you set your mind to do. You become acquainted with and experience your True Woman Self.

It is your choice, however. You can always change your present—and your future—with each of your decisions to be more fully you and to live your potential.

Prepare

In order to be the fullest expression of a happy and healthy you, it is important to tend to your own needs. You can do this by first tending the needs of your body and mind to become strong. This means exercising, reading, studying, eating and sleeping right, and doing all you can to become healthy and alert. It is also essential to seek wisdom, understanding, and spirituality by developing your conscious awareness. Your deeper awareness empowers you in your daily life to act in a manner that promotes your goals, objectives, desires, and dreams.

Pay attention to what is happening inside of you as well as around you. In the process of developing self-awareness, honor yourself and all of your spiritual, mental, and physical gifts and powers. You honor yourself and your gifts when you act on the lessons, insights, hunches, and guidance that you receive. In other words, you honor your gifts by using them. This means paying attention to your body, thoughts, ideas, talents, and abilities and exercising them in a manner that positively affects your daily life.

As you learn your lessons through reflections and meditations, you begin to take more conscious action. Meditation is a wonderful means to focus on what you really think, feel, desire, or doubt about yourself. It is a quiet time that allows you to question why you feel or think about yourself in the way you do. It may mean writing a list of questions to find the deeper truth.

Who, really, are you, anyway? You are not your husband's, partner's, or society's view of you. The real you is not someone else's idea or concept of you. You are *you*!

One helpful tool on your journey is a journal. This not only allows you to keep a record of where you have been and where you are going, but it also gives you evidence of your progress. You might even begin your journal with your commitment to self. Begin by stating that you will commit today to beginning this process of self-discovery. Regardless of where you are in your moon cycle, today you will record what you feel, think, know, or wonder about. You may even write questions that you don't know the answers to, because as you continue to write in your journal, you will find the answers.

It is important to note that journaling is not just writing down what is happening in your daily life—*I got up, I made coffee, I got ready for work*—journaling means taking time to review what you have written and ask yourself important questions. For example: *I awoke and pondered why I stay in this job when I do not enjoy it. Where would I rather be? What do I truly wish or desire to be doing instead of this job that I don't like?*

From this point, you may choose to follow your dream or desire. If you wish to dance, for example, why not take dance lessons? Who offers lessons? When? How much will it cost? Do you need a partner, or is one provided? What time and place and for how long? And yes, you write in your journal about your progress as a dancer!

I find that a weekly review is helpful, although when I first began, it was a year or longer before I went back to look at my journal. When I finally did review my journal entries, I was so surprised and pleased with my progress that I began a monthly review. I later discovered that if I had a lot of entries, a monthly review was too time-consuming, so I began a weekly review.

No matter how you do it, journaling is a beautiful way to see your own growth and the progress you have made, even when life seemed so dismal and uneventful at the time. The more you write and read about yourself, the more you reveal about what you are truly seeking to know. This is a blessing from your inner divine self to you—from your feminine self and your True Woman Self to you.

Be willing to see your own beauty, know your own goodness, and acknowledge your own strengths as you journal.

Breathe Life

The breath of life is given to all of us at birth. But how many of us take it for granted? Perhaps it is now time to breathe in life with knowing and conscious intent.

Did you know that all breath is sacred? It is sacred because it is a gift of life from God/Goddess and your parents. It is the manifestation of your own god-self. Do you know that your breath—each and every inhalation of life into your body—connects you with all other living beings upon this planet? With each breath, you become a part of the Indian prayer for "All Our Relations." This includes star nations, tree nations, rock nations, winged ones, all four-legged animals, all creatures of the air and sea, all creepy crawlers, all of mankind, and Mother Earth herself.

We can all use our breath and breathing patterns to release pent-up emotions and negative feelings without harm to ourselves or others! Let's try it now. Be very still. Hold your breath and allow whatever comes to mind, to your senses, or to your feelings to flow unimpeded. As you do, you may enter other levels of consciousness, other dimensions, or altered states of awareness. This means suddenly finding yourself somewhere else: in a castle, a house, a field, or a park, or by a stream or some other beautiful place. This is an altered state of awareness, because even while you are in this other place, you simultaneously feel yourself or know that you are at home.

Now take three deep breaths. Relax and resume normal breathing, while still focusing on your breath. As you breathe, begin to notice the feelings and sensations of your body. Allow yourself to see, feel, sense, know, taste, hear, and travel within yourself. Did you know that there are specific breathing patterns that allow people to travel into different spiritual realms during deep sleep, dreams, and trances? This type of conscious breathing immerses you in the spiritual realms.

With your breath, you may breathe in the energies of all of life. As you change the rate and rhythm of your breathing, you may tap into other life-forms or enter other dimensions within yourself. Perhaps you will sense your aura or voyage into the universe at large. You control the extent of your adventure into other dimensions. You set the anchor that brings you back here to your earthly reality. Use your breath to travel in joy and connect to the divine energies of the Great Spirit.

Another way to become more aware of your breath and breathing patterns is to center your attention on how you breathe. First, focus on your normal breathing patterns. As you become more aware of what this feels like, ask yourself how you breathe—or don't breathe—when you are happy. How about when you are stressed? How do you breathe or not breathe when you are sad? When you are surprised? How about afraid? Make a mental note of how you are breathing as you feel each of these emotions. Don't try to change your patterns: just become aware of them. You may want to note this in your journal. Then, at a later time, while at home or alone somewhere safe, experiment with different breathing patterns. Note the shifts and variances in how you feel.

Yet another experience you might try is to take a deep breath into your abdomen and hold it for five, ten, or twenty seconds. Then consciously release your breath, exhaling very slowly. Try this a few times. Then try different rapid breaths. Pay attention to your physical response to your breathing at different intervals. How do you feel? Make notes in your journal about all that you feel, think, see, hear, smell, or notice. Pursue the breathing intervals that are most beneficial to you. Don't give up if you don't feel or notice a change. At times, fear may block your awareness of what is happening within you. Keep trying, and allow yourself to relax past the fear.

It is always wise to relax your body before entering any state of stillness. Through your breath and the rhythm of breathing, you have access to the energy called *manna*. Your breath revitalizes each of your cells, your organs, and every part of your body. This revitalization enables you to break the illusion of your current reality, opening other dimensions for you to explore. There are many dimensions within your body, outside of it, in your aura, and within the universe at large.

How Breath Can Change Your Life

In one of my meditations, I wanted to know why I responded to some people in a certain way. This was the focus of my meditation. After the breath exercise, I released myself to experience whatever images might come.

Curiously, I traveled backward in time and saw myself as a small child just beginning school. I was being chastised by my teacher for knowing answers from books that I had not read, because I hadn't yet learned to read. She also chastised me for knowing information and answers that she believed a child could not know.

I realized that to avoid being chastised, I had to hide my knowledge and the information I knew from my teacher. I hid it in my aura! I knew that it was a safe place and she would not look there. Yet I did not then realize that I was hiding my point of access to higher knowing. In fear of that teacher, I forgot where I hid my knowing.

In my meditation, I was able to reexperience what I had done and find out where I had hidden all my knowing as a child, for self-protection. Now, as an adult, I was able to face my child fears and retrieve the information I needed. I adjusted my response to others and was able to again access my own higher knowing.

As you come to realize that all communications are based on the patterns and rhythms of nature, these deeper symbols become readily apparent. As you begin to pay attention at deeper levels to what you are feeling and sensing, and to what you already intuitively know, you may learn to communicate with Nature by *her* rhythms. By doing so, you will also become mindful of your own body's rhythms and language. And as you become aware of these deeper rhythms, you cannot help but become aware of your own beauty.

At such times, you may want to offer a prayer of thanksgiving to Great Spirit for all the wonders and beauty that are revealed to you. You may say your own prayer, or something such as this:

Great Spirit, I give you thanks and appreciation for all the wonders, awesome beauty, and guidance that you have given to me. I praise you and honor you with my willingness to pay attention to the many ways in which you speak to me and guide me throughout my day and life. I also ask forgiveness for my resistance and reluctance to accept the many invitations that you have extended to me throughout my life. I thank you that I have begun my journey to better understand and know you and all the gifts of life. Thank you for all the gifts that life offers to me. And so it is.

Choose Growth

Just as the shaman ritualistically dies to the old as he ventures into new spaces and visions, so also do we die to an older self as we release outdated perceptions. A shaman is willing to let his personal image of himself, his patient, and his world disintegrate; in that openness, he is able to release what binds or brings illness or death to the patient. So too, as you grow into an ever-new vision of yourself, the death of your former personal identity frees you from past limitations. As we proceed in self-knowing, we become balanced and whole within our new selves.

When you go within, look honestly at yourself. Know, name, and deeply feel all that occurs. Then let those emotions wash over and through you. Let your body and spirit tell you what you would really like to do. Allow yourself to feel what it's like doing something that you truly love to do. See yourself doing it. Think about the choices this new option offers. Smell, feel, and touch your surroundings.

For example, if you want to be a dancer, feel the floor under your feet. See yourself reflected in the mirrors as you dance upon the floor of the dance studio. Feel yourself spinning and jumping—feel the energy and fire in the muscles of your legs, feet, arms, and back. Focus on how you hold your body. How do you move as you do what you really love doing? As the awareness of this new you deepens, you begin to release perceptions of yourself in the life you are currently living. Let them go easily, like old shoes—let go of the old, and welcome the new.

I once felt stuck and didn't know what to do, so of course, I went within. I saw my life as it was, and I saw all the things that I found repetitive and unfulfilling. I wanted change so badly. In that feeling, I began to see how it would be necessary to leave the old ways in order to recreate myself and my dreams. I knew I would need to do this away from family and friends. It was clear and easy for me to do once I saw the image and map of what I had to do on my inner screen.

When you resurface from your inner search, you will be a new creation. You will begin to be the person you were created to be. The process and steps will be clear to you.

The purpose of deep inner reflection is to break down former concepts of self-identity that were limiting or untrue. So many of us clutch outdated, useless

16

notions, even though we know they no longer serve us. We know that it is time for introspection when our lives no longer suit us or reflect our personal growth. Recognizing that it is time to let go of old habits and negative friends is our signal that old patterns are already dying.

Remember, if you resist the calls for change, the process is only prolonged. The universe continually calls us to grow and meet our future, but doing so means releasing the negatives that keep us from success. We can always choose to look within ourselves—to see our goodness and acknowledge our talents and abilities. This type of review allows us to turn our lives around. Thus we can enhance our lives and become more open to the opportunities and synchronicities provided for our betterment.

So relax. Accept the mess your life has come to be, by acknowledging and taking responsibility for yourself. Stop fighting with others or blaming them for your misery—such negative efforts will not free you, but will only bury you deeper into misery. Your imaginary obstacles are only illusions, but you are the only one who can break their seeming reality. Indeed, it is only through honest introspection that we can truly choose to live our dreams and dream our lives.

So consciously choose to change! Commit yourself to focusing inward. Look at all of your thoughts, behaviors, wishes, and ideas. Look especially at issues that make you feel vulnerable. Most of all, be willing to see your own beauty, know your own goodness, acknowledge your own strength, use your power, and manifest your grace. Surrender to becoming the real you—a you who is capable of fully giving and receiving love.

Practicing Lessons of Growth

There are many teachers, guides, mentors, and friends who might help us, but it remains our responsibility to practice the lessons we learn. In spiritual learning, we gain in a year what would otherwise take ten years to achieve, for it is accelerated learning, with quantum leaps. When we are ready to take responsibility for our lives, our desired results happen sooner. With each effort, we gain momentum and confidence.

You may want to remind yourself on a daily basis that you are worth the effort, time, and commitment of practicing all your lessons. Remember, when you have completed this task, you will have no one to thank but yourself! No one can ever take from you the power that this process gives to you. In this way, it is a path of freedom. For who could offer you a more treasured gift than that of the self-empowered, free, happy, beautiful, and awesome person that you have become? The choice is yours.

The woman who sees the life she can have and dreams of having opens the door to this possibility. As she reflects on what she needs to do to manifest that new life, she begins to take the necessary steps toward fulfilling her dream. She ends negative relationships, goes back to school, finds a job or other means of self-support, and dares to venture out on her own. She finds support groups and people who will mentor and encourage her on her path to a new life. She trusts her own knowing and builds self-confidence with each effort. She learns to practice her lessons of growth.

Discover the Power Within

Enter the silence to enable your dreams to become realities. Remember that all your answers lie within you.

You are free to seek many alternative ways to achieve your goals and spiritual direction. Use your feminine receptive energies to focus on inner knowing and allow clarity to rise and emerge. Be your own advisor. Regain your authority, because no one knows what is right for you better than you do.

Be attentive to your behaviors and your thoughts. Where are you in your process? Are you just coming into your ideas and plans of what you wish to do, or are you refining them? Have you completed your project? By knowing where you are, you will know how to proceed. Look to see and understand the cues offered to you by your body, and pay attention to symbols presented in everyday life. Everything is a symbol or cue for what to do next.

You might ask yourself: Where are your aches and pains? Where do your fat cells collect? What part of you hungers? Do your ears twitch? Do you feel as if you need to run or bolt? What is your body telling you or asking of you? For example, if your lower leg is itching, is there something in your understanding that needs to be reviewed or reconsidered? Was this leg previously injured by someone who gave you some useful advice that you ignored? Is it now time to reconsider that advice?

One way I learned to read my bodily responses was by applying related ideas through common sense. For instance, my legs were under me; I stood on them. So I interpreted images that involved my legs as having to do with my understanding. Thus, images of legs in my dreams and meditations indicated to me that I was addressing my own understanding of things or how I saw or perceived something. The question of understanding became the focus of the message from the dream, prayer, or meditation.

You can similarly let your body, mind, soul, and emotions lead you. Trust the power within yourself, but be open to receiving inner guidance from Spirit too.

As you contemplate the symbols and answers that come, you begin to trust that you really *do* know what is best for you. Trust that the answers you seek are always available to you if you ask and look within. Your body always offers the answers you are seeking.

Remember, "Spirit" does not mean what your church is telling you, but what the godliness within you is revealing from your own divine source, from your center, which is created in the image and likeness of God.

For example, the title for this book comes from a time when I went to visit friends at a Catholic university in New York City. We sat around one evening for a meditative prayer that we easily shared. We turned down the lights and lit a few candles. We entered the silence, did our deep breathing together, and then each entered our own individual meditation.

No sooner than entering the beginning of the quiet time, I found myself far away in consciousness. Soaring over the Southwest desert, I could see clearly for miles; the red sandstone buttes below were magnificent and powerful. The desert sand, dotted by cactus sprouting here and there, shifted in a warm summer breeze. The sky was immensely blue.

I was way out there. I couldn't tell if I was riding the eagle or one of the eagles, but we were soaring. Like being in a hot-air balloon, there was no sensation of movement. I was the movement, I was the bird, I was the universe; and I could see and know forever.

From eternity, Earth was a beautiful presence to behold. It was a moment and an eternity. I was peaceful, filled with love, wisdom, wonder, and awe. It was oh-so-easy to soar, to allow the thermals to support and carry me, to circle as long and wide as I pleased. God, Spirit, and Wisdom were everywhere, in the breeze, hearing and answering our prayers and loving us. I knew that I belonged there and loved to be there. It was home, and I was free. I loved it.

Flying Within

You too can have a flying experience as described above. Such states are easily available as you practice meditation, deep reflection, and prayer. To "launch" yourself, you might follow a guided meditation with a friend. Or you can easily make your own by reading the above passage about the eagle flight into a recorder. Then, replay the tape as you enter a meditative state. You may want to first prepare your space by lighting candles and dimming the lights. Try this exercise several times, on different evenings. As you progress, choose to ever more vividly see yourself or feel yourself soaring with the eagles. You may vary the imagery by soaring over some place that you have already been, some place you find safe, lovely, warm, and inviting. Once the tape is over, return to your room and make notes in your journal about your experiences, feelings, and insights.

Accept Guidance

Changes are first born of spirit. It is only after a spiritual change is made that it flows through your intuition and into conscious awareness. Spirit enables the seeds of knowing to enter your mental, physical, and emotional realities. So be alert in order to receive the messages available to you. Use your intuition to discern the message.

In the process of discerning the messages of your life, commune often with your guides. They await your invitation and the opening of your heart. Take time to sense them, feel their presence, and listen to their nudges and cues. Jump right in—don't wait and wonder about it.

For example, one day while jogging, I heard the sound of tiny bells tinkling to my left. I could see someone in my peripheral vision. He was a young Indian male dressed in buckskin clothing and moccasins. I focused on the sound of the bells. They sounded like "miracle bells"—tiny bells of painted enamel, about a quarter inch in diameter, found in Native American craft stores.

I recalled the sound of the miracle bells on my prayer wand—a wand that I created, decorated, and used as part of my morning prayer and prayer dance. Holding my focus on the sound of the bells, I found that I could more clearly see my guide. I instinctively knew him to be Wind Spirit Guide, and I called him by that name. I thanked him for joining me and welcomed him into my life.

Meet Your Guides

Spirit guides may become more apparent to as you more deeply reflect, meditate, and pray. They may first appear simply as feelings, notions, ideas, or an inner knowing. With practice, however, you may come to know their individual personalities, tones, sounds, silence, and styles.

Allow your guides to take you on journeys into the past and future and into different aspects of your present life. Your guides offer truths that will lead you to your path, teaching you all that you need to know. They will sing to you of ancient knowledge.

Honor, love, and respect your spirit guides, who have stood by in total readiness for your invitation to proceed. Bless them and thank them, for they have exercised great patience with you, and they love you.

I first became aware of my guides when I began to pay serious attention to my life. At that time, I had started to journal, and I noticed recurring themes in both my nightly dreams and the events of my daily life. As I focused on these themes and curious observations, I began to discern messages, clues, and cues. With practice and a bit of time, I began to recognize the voices and tones of different guides.

The next awakening for me was to recognize my guides themselves. I did that by focusing on the various beings who appeared in my dreams and meditations. Sometimes the same person or persona will reappear in several dreams or meditations. When this happens, stop and ask who is present. Ask this being if he or she is one of your guides. When I finally did this, I was ready, open, and willing to accept help and direct guidance from my guides.

Reclaim Your Spiritual Powers

With Spirit, you can defy your fears and human frailties. In Spirit, you are confident and self-assured. With spiritual intervention, you are capable of all things.

This is the assurance you need as you begin to break down old memories, to free yourself from limiting misconceptions and misperceptions of self. As you face your fears, *know* that you are safe. Know too that you are the one who sets the limits as to which fears you will address. The degree to which you face your fears is the degree to which you enable yourself to address ever greater fears. In this way, fear no longer rules your life.

To reclaim your spiritual powers, begin by setting your own stage. Create a sacred space for yourself in your home or another peaceful, quiet space. Unplug the phone and turn down the lights. You may want to light candles, use incense, or smudge yourself and your prayer or meditation area. Do some preliminary deep breathing, or simply take three deep breaths, slowly exhaling, to settle down into yourself.

It is important to consciously prepare yourself as well as your prayer area. Clarify your intent and desire for this time of quiet, then begin to enter your own silence. You may intone, sing, chant *Om*, or make any other sounds to calm yourself. This may be as simple as breathing deeply and sighing on the exhale, releasing in sound whatever you are feeling.

Using your mental, physical, and emotional selves, ask to reach your spirit guides and ask for them to reach you. Consciously collect the memories that you wish to work with and pull them into your physical and mental space. As you work with your memories, you may sometimes notice that your guides will warp, exaggerate, or expose the hidden meanings of the images that you carry from your life experiences. Or they may mirror back to you ways in which you have deceived yourself, offering changes that you may need to make. In the midst of the exercise, you may realize that you are in an altered state of consciousness. Quite often within this state, you can learn who you are and why you do the things that you do, or why you have the behavior patterns that you have.

Memories that you have not previously recalled may flood your mind, or perhaps images from your past or past lives will be exposed. The responsibility to understand the images, symbols, and message is yours. If you do not work to try to understand your own images and symbols, your guides will not do it for you. They will not do your homework.

To figure out your symbolic language—and it *is* a new language—it is necessary to pay attention to what you think, feel, sense, and know inside. This is not the quick response of mind, but the quiet voice within. This "still, small voice" speaks of the impressions you sense, the visual images you see, and the verifications from your inner self and inner knowing. Let your body do the talking, not your mind!

In these focused moments of reflection, you can retrieve many memories: old memories, forgotten memories, past-life memories, and others that you may have hidden from yourself. It is also your responsibility to retrieve the lessons and messages from those memories. It is not about who you were in some past life, but rather what you learned and what lessons you carry over into this life. In such reflections, you may recall your spiritual powers and claim them in this lifetime—this time, this place, and this body. You alone are responsible for recalling, remembering, and reclaiming all of your own spiritual powers.

Did you know that you can even change a memory in the same way that you can change a dream? Perhaps you will see a blockage and intuitively know what to do to change that image. As you do, you will change your life and your understanding of life.

For example, perhaps you recall yourself as a child afraid of dogs. Go back to your childhood, to that time when you first became afraid of dogs. Perhaps it began with what someone said or thought about dogs, or an actual experience you had with dogs. After reflection on what was said, heard, felt, thought, or implied, you can decide for yourself as an adult whether or not this is still valid for you. If it is not, you can change the memory of your child-self with your adult knowledge and spiritual discernment.

During this type of reflective exercise, your purpose is to free yourself from blockages and bondage so that spirit can freely flow through you. Your goal is to expand your spiritual being while in your physical body. This is not an exercise to leave or reject your body, but to spiritually enhance your body to become more spiritually aware on all levels—mentally, physically, emotionally, and spiritually.

Although you might leave your physical body as you advance on your spiritual journey, it is only to retrieve information and bring that knowledge back to your mental, physical self.

Be aware of your limitations, however. Trust your knowing and your intuition to let you know what to do and when to stop. In reclaiming your inner knowing, you will always be able to discern what you need to do next.

Notice Symbols

Have you ever been stopped in your tracks by the sudden vision of someone or something that pierces the veils of consciousness and speaks directly to your heart? Say you are walking along, and you suddenly notice a small, bright-eyed child at a bus stop or in a crowd. Even though the child is just being a child, the vision radiates a sense of God/Goddess to you. Do you walk on, or do you take this in at a deeper level, accepting it as an invitation for you to examine what the image of innocence or bright eyes means to you?

Most people don't look beyond the image. In failing to do so, they foolishly disregard what intuition reveals about their true feelings. Perhaps this bright-eyed child is a symbol of something you need or want to address on a subconscious level. Why not go there to look, feel, ponder, and open yourself to the experience of knowing something more about yourself?

For example, does the image of this child's bright eyes tell you that you are keeping your power activated, ready for action, but hidden? Do the images around you reflect a part of you that needs to be observed in more detail? Do the events happening around you mirror a hidden aspect of yourself? Is there some part of you patiently waiting for you to remember or recall that it is there? Is there some part of you waiting to be released or to have its power harnessed in your life?

Note what you need to work on. Acknowledge the problems that you see, such as anger, attitude, self-negation, or denial. Recognize the work that yet needs to be addressed. Prepare to go forward, but take time to realize that all you need is within you. It simply awaits your call to action as you recognize and interpret the messages held within the symbols of nature, people, books, and events around you. Recognize and appreciate this inner pageantry, for this is the movie of your life. Pay attention and discover what it is telling you about you!

For example, allow yourself to see the part of you that wants to be loved as a woman. See the part of you that is missing because you projected her out of yourself for safekeeping during childhood. Do other women mirror your feminine image back to you? Does the image of certain women upset you, irritate you, and make you squirm, or enrage you? Do you deny their beauty? Or do they help you to see that you too have a radiantly beautiful smile? That you too are shapely, intelligent, invigorating, exciting, wonderful, spiritual, witty, charming, brilliant, and powerful?

Do children who freely give love and exude joy and intelligent, spontaneous expressions upset you or make you smile in remembrance? Perhaps that whiny little girl you notice is a reflection of your own fear. Does her image show you that you need love, but don't know how to get it or receive it? Or that you know something is wrong but don't know how to express yourself, or even what you feel? Are you rejecting the love that you so desperately want and need because you are afraid you won't get it?

If we suffer from abandonment issues, it's because, more than anything else, we feel abandoned. If we feel left alone in a hostile, violent, lonely world, we may cry, whine, and feel sorry for ourselves. In that state, we drive those who would love us away by the denial of our true feelings. We cry out for love. Yet love naturally flows toward love, because like attracts like. Love naturally flows toward us, because we are lovable and loving just as we are.

In truth, an abundance of love energy is bouncing around the universe, freely available for you to gather, utilize, and incorporate at will. Your guides are present to help you gather information, knowledge, and wisdom, as well as to form conclusions and plans of action. Your guides are ready to help you figure out symbols, images, clues, and cues in order to unlock the secrets of your life. As you reflect on this valuable information, the lessons and power put on hold by your own self-deception and self-imposed limits will be revealed to you. You will recognize the way life, spirit, and your inner self speak to you through symbols and images at all times.

Finding the Message

One easy and interesting way to learn more about symbols is to consider the people and events around you as messages to yourself. Become enthralled with everyone and anyone who catches your attention, for whatever reason. Begin to see these events and people as symbols sent from your spiritual self to your conscious self as an aid to self-discovery.

Look at other people as they walk or sit and take note of what their image and behavior says to you. Take in elements such as neatness, disarray, color, posture, stride, height, and weight as symbols. Note these distinctions and observations in your journal. As you do, continue to reflect on what this tells you about yourself. What is your spiritual self trying to tell you?

Study Mirrors

To further your process of self-discovery, another method of facing inner issues is to do the following meditation exercise with a mirror. You can do this alone by looking deeply into your own eyes in the mirror, or you can look into the eyes of a partner. In either case, settle yourself with some calming breaths. Breathe deeply, relax, and focus on your breathing. Focus your intent, and be open to receiving the messages your inner guides offer. Allow yourself to accept all feelings, thoughts, images, and symbols that rise.

Now focus on whatever image you see in your eyes in the mirror or in the eyes of your partner. Those eyes will mirror back to you issues you need to address. Why? Because they reflect what is held in your soul and body.

Whatever comes up—fears, intimacy, discomfort, nervousness, or beauty—is what you are to meditate upon. Meditation is focused concentration, so trust your intuition to teach and lead you. See the ageless beauty and love of God radiating from within you. Look at your own glorious god-self—that part of you that is created in the image and likeness of God.

Sometimes we have the most difficulty seeing our own beauty. At first, you may recoil and resent the intense gaze or close proximity of another person in your space. However, you are always free to acknowledge your own feelings before proceeding as instructed. You will generally find this exercise to be quite informative and rewarding, regardless of any initial feelings and thoughts to the contrary.

Focus on all aspects of your responses. How do you feel physically, mentally, emotionally, and spiritually? How does your body react to the other person looking so intently into your eyes? How do you react to your own eyes in the mirror, or to the image of your body? What do you sense, feel, smell, hear, think, taste, or intuit? Don't be alarmed by strange or unexpected images. If you are frightened, take a deep breath and know that you can stop merely by averting your eyes, if necessary. It is fine to resume once you have regained composure.

Trust whatever your body is saying to you. Your body is more honest than your mind. At the same time, don't discount your mind. Instead, make peace with it. Invite your mind to come along as a silent observer.

What We See: An Experience

I once did this eye exercise with a friend. We locked eyes and gazed deeply. Suddenly, my friend became frightened and asked to stop. Of course, I stopped and asked if she wanted to talk about it. She was at first reluctant to say what she observed in my eyes. After chatting a few moments, she said that she had seen a very scary-looking being in my eyes. We laughed and made some jokes about the various aspects of my being that could be expressing themselves and seeking to be recognized and acknowledged.

Once my partner felt comfortable, she asked to resume the exercise. It ended quite well for both of us. We shared what we saw in each other's eyes. I accepted and loved this scary part of myself, and I thanked her for revealing herself to me. I realized she had been born with some difficulty in her life, and I loved her as a survivor who blessed me with endurance and stamina. I sent her love and appreciation. I also thanked my partner for permitting me to gaze into her eyes and soul.

Face Your Fear

It is always wise to be aware of any fear or resistance that you feel. Why? Because your fear can set you free. It's true: if you face your fears, they will melt before you, and you will be released from their grip. If you run from fear, however—or if you have been chased and hounded in the dark by fear, or by some unknown, fearsome, threatening force—you will only fuel your own fearful illusions. Fear can easily change the innocent games and remarks of others into threats and conflict.

Unchecked fear will often cause you to take evasive or defensive actions in response to otherwise neutral stimuli. You may sense danger where no danger exists. You may fall prey to the fear tactics of religions and propaganda, for both feed on fear and manipulate through fear. Fear has the power to dissolve your bones. It can cause you to lose control over your will and actions. Fear deforms your feelings; it contaminates your thinking.

If you fear that certain people are gossiping about you, you will be fearful whenever you see those people talking. They may well be discussing business, a movie, or a game plan for the day or evening, but your fears will interpret the image of them talking as gossip about you. You will imagine all sorts of negative language, name-calling, jeopardy, or threats. Unless you confront your fear (for example, by approaching those people), you will never know the truth of what was said. You will instead harbor ill feelings or greater fear because of what you feared may have been said.

Yet all you have to do is relax, feel your sense of self, and separate your feelings and self from that fear. How to do this? Start by feeling the panic, fear, and reactive behaviors while simultaneously remembering the stillness of your inner self. Walk into this still center. Don't fight the fear, but allow the fear to wash over you. As you feel it, you will overcome it, and it will melt away. By doing this in a consistent manner, you will find your strength and power returning to you in ever-greater amounts. Soon, fear will never control you again.

Facing Fear

When I was twelve years old, in school, I once observed a priest slap a girl fully across her face. He hit her so hard that she had whiplash. I spontaneously and instinctively yelled, "You keep your hands off of her!"

The priest rushed over to my desk. Looking down, towering over me, he yelled, "What did you say?"

In absolute fear and trepidation, I stood up by my desk, looked him in the eye, and responded, "I said, you keep your hands off of her."

Although I knew that he could strike me in the same manner, I stood up to him and repeated my spontaneous utterance. For an eternal moment, he glared at me with red eyes, and his hand raised, ready to strike me. Then, just as suddenly as he had approached my desk, he departed the classroom. He never again slapped another student after that day.

Looking back, I can no longer feel the fear, but I knew it did wash over me in a mighty wave as he approached my desk. In fact, that wave of fear not only washed over me, but through me and out my feet by the time he reached my desk.

This is what facing your fears allows you to do. It was a David and Goliath moment.

Sculpt Your Own Image

It is your choice. You alone decide whether or not you want to change your present and future and, with each of your choices, to become more fully you.

There may be times when you may feel unprepared for continuing the exercise of clearing old blockages and moving past fear. In spite of your doubts, however, trusting yourself and your guides will make it easier to proceed. You may even find that you are suddenly in a rush to discover more about yourself, and you may be directed to pay more attention to your exterior life in order to gain balance in your physical life.

The journey of self-discovery is an adventure that can be exciting, scary, dark, bright, and full of the unexpected. We may be asked to reexamine areas of our inner selves that we feel we have already inspected. It may be with reluctance that we review certain areas, only to find new hidden treasures.

The process is like sculpting a new image. We let the material tell us what to create, and we are both the artist and the stone. Feel, listen, and sense what is to be created. Let the anticipation and expectancy rise high above your current capacity to understand, until your feelings overflow into life. It is an exciting journey into the self that allows us to rediscover our inner beauty. Like a diamond in the rough, beauty may not be apparent until we have removed some of the hardened thoughts and misperceptions.

At times, we may feel that we have already examined our spiritual foundations and mental self-images, or that we have challenged our beliefs and conclusions. Yet we often need to readjust exterior responses and behavior patterns to be in accord with our new understanding, so we may need to return to the interior for more work. We might resist and claim that we do not need to spend more time reviewing our beliefs or rechecking our concepts, ideas, laws, and rules. In spite of these feelings, however, we must proceed from time to time with reexamination.

On review, we may note that, like the sculptor, our creation is slightly "off" because of something we did or did not do. While we didn't see it before, now we do. And so, with patience and a clearer vision, we reshape the material and create an even more beautiful person. Keep in mind that in art, mistakes are not negative endings; rather, they are the points of departure into new expressions or visions not previously considered. We too can review and recreate. We are always free to venture into and create new expressions of self.

Transmute the Negative

Do you want to transmute your negative energies into the fiery passion that is often called zeal? In order to do this, you must learn to change your mental, physical, and emotional awareness.

For example, when Native Americans pray for "All Our Relations," we are acknowledging the oneness of all things. We are reaffirming that we all breathe the same air and live in joy and sorrow, excitement and numbness. We all are born and die. And despite racial prejudices or religious beliefs, we are all one in Spirit; we all share the same human experiences.

When we begin to understand the balance in all things and honor the divine energy that creates wholeness, we may begin to know that we are children of the universe. By working to accept all parts and aspects of ourselves, we begin to change our negative energies into a positive, creative force. With that force, we find ourselves becoming more passionate, creative, and resolute in following our dreams. Our intellects become stimulated and powerful, and we take charge of our lives. We may become charismatic and wise. We may even become aware of our connection to Great Spirit.

To do this, however, we must openly and honestly face all of our inner demons and darkness. We face our shadows by accepting and looking at the parts of ourselves that we don't like or appreciate. Take a moment now and look. As you do, seek an understanding of why you think or feel this way about that part of yourself.

The experience may bring temporary discomfort and self-doubt, and you may even try to talk yourself out of change. You may fall back into the rut you were in, because it is familiar and easy. Perhaps you will blame others: your spouse or children; your job or financial situation; your education; or your lack of wealth. But all these and more are only justifications for not looking within and facing that inner self.

We can choose to look within. Remember, we have already survived everything in our lives until now, and we can proceed with courage and daring. If we choose to remain in our rut until some outside force startles us into an inner search, that too will work. This might include loss of employment, deaths of loved ones, illness, divorce or the end of a relationship, an accident, meeting someone new, or simply discovering a new idea or book.

Experience suggests that it's easier to surrender to self early. Then we can become whole sooner and stop the sham that has been our life as defined by others. For example, if you dropped out of high school because your friends did, you may find it difficult to find a job. Perhaps you fell in with others doing drugs or alcohol. As a result, you may find yourself constantly falling short of your dreams. But once you decide to change or to do something different (such as getting a GED or seeking training or a mentor), your life path changes.

You don't have to do it alone. You can invite a friend, spouse, or lover to join you or help. Or perhaps you want to join a group or talk with a counselor. You might also choose to simply talk with your spiritual guides from within yourself. Great Sprit never fails us, even when we choose not to listen. The spiritual guidance is always there, and it will always be true from that place within each of us where our god-self dwells.

Transmute the Negative

Begin the process of transmuting the negative by seeking, knowing and accepting your oneness in the universe. You do this by realizing you are connected to all of creation. As you honestly look at your life, actions, thoughts, ideas, and notions, question why you do the things you do. Why didn't you take action in a particular situation? What were the fears, doubts, and discomfort that stopped you?

Look at the times you felt like you failed. Now go deeper into what you were feeling and thinking at the time. As you look back, you will have new insights into choices that you could have made. This review enables you to separate your desires from your fears. You will be better equipped to view your abilities and capabilities in spite of your fear. This type of review allows you to transmute the negatives in your life into positive energies and new possibilities. Give it a try!

Appreciate the Vastness

From time to time, you may need to take a break from your inner work and soul searching. Instead, you might want to focus on your exterior physical and mental levels, noticing the change of your behaviors. You may seek some logical understanding of what is happening with you. You may read spiritual texts in search of a more conscious understanding of your spiritual development. In reviewing all that has happened in your journey by reading your journal, you may also be amazed to realize how much time you have spent in mental, logical searches for your spiritual self and God in the past.

As you come back from some exterior appreciation of how far you have traveled, you might notice that mental and physical questions have become less meaningful, or may not even make any sense anymore. You might even begin to see your night dreams and the world around you as symbols. Even written words may become visual symbols.

For example, you may dream that you use a particular word that you normally do not use. As you reflect on your dream, look up the word in a dictionary and consider all of its meanings, and think about how they reflect on your life. Even words you hear on a daily basis may suddenly sound different or carry a new meaning or nuance that you hadn't previously considered.

In addition, mental concepts may take on different meanings. Spiritually, you may sense how to enhance and expand those concepts without limits. Remember, logic may take you from *A* to *B* to *C,* but spiritual knowing will take you from *A* to infinity. Thus you may realize, intuit, know, and seek new ways of thinking, viewing, and opening to alternatives not previously considered.

In time, you may realize the vastness of your spiritual knowing. It is like moving from silent movies into a high-tech movie production. One day you are at your maximum mental and physical expression in silent movies, and in the next instant (via spiritual incorporation of right and left brains), you are able to perform multimedia expressions and special effects without effort.

As you surrender to the imagery and symbols of your life, you may become lost in the spiritual vastness. That is why it is important to center yourself and trust your abilities. This allows you to float with joy in that mystery.

Enthusiastically and with complete abandon, we can surrender to spiritual vastness. As we dissolve limited mental presumptions and logical assumptions, we yield to inner knowing. We are suddenly able to make easy connections between symbols and their meanings. We may see and understand the principles of quantum physics. We may even realize the ease with which we can make quantum leaps into our spiritual future and simultaneously be in our physical and mental bodies.

To encourage this process, you might begin by doing right-left brain exercises. A simple version of this involves drawing a line down the center of a piece of paper and continuously moving your vision in a zigzag pattern across the line—left to right, right to left, and so on. You might also practice moving your eyes in a horizontal figure eight symbol, again left to right and back again, as though tracing the frames of a pair of glasses with your eyes.

Can you imagine what will happen when you "wake up" and realize just how vast you truly are? On some level, you have known this all your life! This was how you knew the answers to problems without having gone through the logical steps or instructions. This was how you experienced astral travel and out-of-body episodes. Perhaps it is now time to forgive yourself, to let go of erroneous assumptions and presumptions about yourself and others. Mistaken bygones are not worth the time it takes to regret them. You have bigger and better things to do!

Expand Your Boundaries

I once worked for a man who had me working eighteen hours a day. Week after week, it got progressively worse. As I did not have relief staff, I even began working weekends to keep up with the demand. I ended up with an ulcer, so I requested time off for medical reasons. My boss said no! I then asked for two weeks off, and he again said no.

As we spoke, I suddenly realized that I didn't need to do this. I told my boss, "I'll give you two weeks' notice." Before he could respond, I added, "No, I've changed my mind. I quit, effective immediately. Please have my check ready in two days."

My boss was incredulous. He said, "You can't do that! What are you going to do?" I responded that I didn't exactly know. Perhaps I would begin by taking an extended vacation and figure it out for myself. I knew that I had to find my own dream, and to find that dream, I needed to stop living his.

Expanding the boundaries that surround our comfort zones often happens in a manner that is totally unexpected. We may find ourselves doing things that we thought we would never do, such as taking a stand in front of a boss, or spending time with people we thought we would not enjoy. Perhaps we may go to a movie that did not appeal to us, or read a book that seemed tedious, but was recommended by a friend. Yet, as we follow these exterior suggestions, we begin to observe and incorporate subtle changes within our beings.

Our true goals are realized from within. We are always where we are supposed to be. Still, our circumstances are constantly challenging us: Are we where we desire to be? Is this the life that we've dreamed of living?

If our answers are not in line with what we want, it is up to us to do something to break the illusion. Say, *No, I don't care to do that anymore. No, I've changed my mind. I'd rather turn left and see what lies beyond the hill. I will indeed go back to school and take those classes that are of particular interest to me. I will resign my secure job with benefits and seek employment in a field that really excites me, regardless of the pay. Then I will throw out all unnecessary belongings, find a new place to live, or simply learn to stand on my head so I can see the world differently.*

We deserve—and can attain—the very best of our dreams. As we welcome the abundance, we attain the joys of life that are our birthright. To begin to gather and receive these blessings, we need to consciously pay attention to our lives and to ourselves.

Small Ways to Expand

Each morning, say hello to yourself in the mirror as you would a new friend. Then deliberately, consciously—in full mental, spiritual, emotional, and physical awareness—pay attention to what you do and say throughout the day.

For example, take time to write notes to yourself about all that is good and enjoyable about your job. List all that is negative. Can you change the good into better? Can you change the negatives into positives? Do you want to? If not, are you willing to seek other employment or training, or to go back to school? Are you willing to find a mentor? With your notes and the help of your guides, begin to design your dream job.

You can step into your spiritual role, focus on the force and power of your abilities, and appreciate the expanded boundaries of your comfort zone. As you proceed, realize that all you need is within you. Prepare to laugh and enjoy the wonders and gifts that are freely showered upon you. Dance with joy! Be overwhelmed with magnificence and power as you float on love.

Awaken to the Spiritual

To open ourselves to the wholeness of cosmic consciousness, we must willingly experience all things without resistance. To do this, we must also trust that all things are of equal value in the universe. We can develop the capacity to undertake this task through the complete understanding, acceptance, and balance of our inner male and female selves as spiritual energy.

Inner balancing enables us to realize that we are universal beings. This calm awareness creates a spiritual fire or creative energy that makes use of and accepts all aspects of self. In the process, we create passion, desire, vitality, and physical strength. Our efforts to become more spiritually open give us ambition, creativity, dreams, and the ability to resolve issues that confront us on an emotional level. Our intellect is enhanced, our charisma is released, and we assume roles of leadership with courage, foresight, and power.

Our fire energy—that energy that burns and builds in our solar plexus—is generated by the life energies we create as we grow and develop spiritually. This energy is uniquely expressed in our wisdom, understanding, and outward wholeness. Our connection to Great Spirit becomes deep and fervent with our building fire energy.

It is our will, conscious intention, and desire that fuels how we proceed. As we consciously choose to be or do what we intend, we begin to transform every thought, action, or desire to attain our wholeness and dreams. We do this by taking responsibility to transmute our negative energies into the positive power or fire that we need. We must do this now! We must remove the masks that we have hidden behind. We must free our ability to change limiting aspects of our present circumstances and stop hiding in the shadows of our beings. Do you dare to look at yourself from the viewpoint of your all-knowing inner self?

For example, you may already recognize that your present life and home are safe but nonproductive. This is often a call to release the façade of present identity. As you move beyond the illusion that has held you bound for all these years, you open to your true self. This new, real you will create, express, and dream of new rhythms for living. She will release your soul so that you may connect even more deeply with God and Great Spirit.

This new True Woman Self immerses us in the waters of Great Spirit. We come to know that we are loved, accepted, recognized, and called by Great Spirit into our divine wholeness. Thus she teaches us to dance our personal dance of power, showing us how to incorporate transmuted energies into the universal forces that were always meant to be ours.

True Woman Self leads us into and through greater challenges via ideas, jobs, and accomplishments. She leads us to college, marriage, divorce, independence, or child-rearing. Your True Woman Self may lead you to run for office, or step down from office, or do something completely different with your life.

The vastness of god-love is never too much or too little, for its source is eternally abundant. As you enter and surrender yourself to that spiritual cleansing, you may become aware of your own unkind or unloving behaviors. You see them clearly, but without guilt or shame. You may now know they are inappropriate and that you do not wish to continue in that negative manner.

It is so clear—such a deep knowing!—that this experience may change us forever. We may not resume our old ways, because there is no energy within us that will permit us to proceed in that direction. Whenever we recall our spiritual cleansing, we may be reminded of the depth of that change. We may also know how profoundly we might regret repeating any of the old negative behaviors.

We may even seek to apologize to those we have previously offended. We must, however, check to see that we are not misleading ourselves back into shame or guilt behaviors. It is important to question whether or not we are acting from old, fear-based responses. Are we afraid that God will punish us? Are we just putting on a show for someone, or are we being led by our knowing? We must be aware of our personal knowing and what our personal change means to us.

So be aware of all your habits—both the obvious and the subtle ones. This enables you to live freely and fully in your experience of self. Realize which beliefs and behaviors are truly your own. Have you assumed the ideas, thoughts, or notions of your spouse, friends, enemies, or lovers? Are these thoughts and beliefs in agreement with your spiritual knowing and experience, or simply those of your church, family, neighbors, or society?

When you have a spiritual awakening, you are responsible for living in accordance with what you know to be true. This means being spiritually responsible for *yourself*—not for someone else. You cannot really "save" someone else; after all, spirit speaks to you only about you. You are not my savior, nor am I yours. You are invited to proceed in the god-love that only you experience. As you live in it and surrender to it, you begin to change.

Once the invitation is accepted, we may realize how foolish we have been, running from the best in us. When we surrender to Spirit, we may see and know all of our own false starts. We may see and understand how we have sabotaged all of our own best efforts. We may both laugh and cry with tears of joy, release, and relief.

As we surrender to the moment and focus upon Spirit, we become aware of ourselves. In that self-consciousness, we begin to realize who or what Spirit is. We begin to know the immensity of love.

Be of One Mind

Do you know that you can turn your darkness into light? When you connect your intuitive, spiritual side with your physical, mental side, you can proceed as a team, moving together as a unit in love, friendship, and trust. You might begin this process by accepting the unique gifts of each side of your brain.

For example, you may realize that your left brain likes to say, "But what if?" even if this includes negative, fearful what-ifs. In comparison, your right brain may see potential, possibilities, positives, and obstacles as challenges. It is important to not take either side for granted.

If your thinking brain and your intuition hide from one another, seek the hidden one. Don't let fear or ignorance, pride or greed separate you, nor jealousies or feelings of inferiority. Instead, accept love, kindness, compassion, tenderness, beauty, grace, power, and innocence as gifts from Great Spirit. For example, when someone offers a compliment, accept it graciously. Don't challenge or counter the compliment by saying it really wasn't that good.

Love, respect, honor, and appreciate the gifts from both sides. If you stumble or fall into a rut in either your right-brain or left-brain functions, lovingly pick up that side and nurse yourself back to health and wholeness. Don't let "what if" fears keep you from trying something new; at the same time, don't proceed prematurely without a plan or in blind faith without assessing the skills needed for a task. As you stay in accordance with your left and right brains, you proceed as one mind.

Live a Prayer

As you proceed upon your journey of transformation, you may have many achievements to rejoice in and celebrate with friends and family. In your explorations, remember to thank your guides and express gratitude for the lessons learned. You may also want to release those guides who have completed their time of teaching. As you do so, new guides will come to assist you.

Although you may be learning rapidly and making great leaps in knowing, do not become arrogant or let your mind fool you into a false sense of superiority. Doing so may land you in serious trouble. You may find yourself running down the path of ego only when it is too late.

We have legions of spirit guides, much like a spiritual family, awaiting our invitation to help us on our journey. In many instances, our guides will humble us with their wisdom by revealing the magnificent and awesome gifts and powers that we have so long buried and hidden from ourselves. At times, we might pray or ask for their forgiveness of our failure to acknowledge, recognize, or accept our true selves despite their relentless efforts to awaken us to who we truly are. As long as we refuse to acknowledge the lessons, our guides are bound to us.

If we place ourselves in exile, our guides too are exiled from their next level of being. Our guides, like us, are on a continuous journey into greater wholeness and glory. When we understand that and their patience with us, we may be truly humbled.

Indeed, our guides humble us with their patience and joy, their sense of celebration of our lives. Knowing this, we may find ourselves singing praise for God, Great Spirit, and our guides. As we give thanks, we may dance with joy. We may learn to pray and to express gratitude. We may then learn what prayer truly is—and that our lives are a prayer. When our lives become a conscious prayer, we may open to yet another level of spiritual awareness.

We may realize this life prayer in any event. For example, perhaps you are helping a friend move to a new residence. As you clean and pack, be present to her as a living prayer. In doing so, you not only share the cleaning and packing, but also the memories, tears, or joy. Celebrate the treasures she keeps, gives away, or throws out. Give thanks for her, with your very being, in every action, thought, and effort.

Your life becomes a prayer when your thoughts and actions are filled with giving gratitude, appreciation, and thanks without effort. When you have labored long on a task, allow yourself to feel grateful upon its completion, with appreciation for the opportunity. When you give thanks for a loving brother who died, you open yourself to the depths of the blessing of his time here. Your life is a prayer as you give love, thanks, appreciation, and gratitude for all the wonders, people, and events of your life.

A Personal Prayer of Thanks

When my brother Ritchie died, I entered the depths and darkness of my being. I hurt until I was numb.

And yet, it was only by entering into the depth of that pain and numbness that I was able to begin to heal. It was only there that I was able to first feel the true fullness of God in the depths of my being and soul. It was from those very depths of pain that love, light, and joy once again began to shine. In the process, no part of me was left untouched by God/Goddess/Great Spirit.

I know now that it was only when I fully faced my own pain, darkness, and sorrow that my life could again become a prayer and song unto God. I could then give thanks and celebrate the joy of having such a brother for the time he was here.

I still feel the love, joy, and wonder of his life. And I still give thanks, appreciation, and gratitude for him daily.

Honor Spiritual Law

Know the power of balance within your soul. Seek the stillness within, even when all about you is in turmoil, and stay in the eye of the storm. If you keep questioning and facing the darkness within yourself, you will continue to change into the new you. Guided by intuition and spirit, you will open to the unknowable mysteries of the universe. You may be able to break the illusions of reality, attaining the ability to create new realities and go in and out of dimensions freely.

In this way, we may pass into new incarnations with full memories of our past lives. This is the power of change that comes from introspection. It enables us to simultaneously see the past, present, and future. We may likewise apprehend inner and outer realities at the same time.

By looking within ourselves, we may open to allow Spirit to guide us to our own best good and the good of all. We may then speak in a powerful voice when we address issues that are out of balance, unjust, or unfair. We may look at the world with one eye in the Higher Realms and one on the Earth plane. We may be present both here and there. As we allow personal integrity to be our guide, we stand in our convictions with compassion.

By using our gifts and powers of knowing, we may aid in creating a world of peace and understanding. Our very being may call ourselves and others into action. As always, we need to be honest with ourselves and others; we need to stay alert, pay attention, and be ready to act. We come to see the importance of clearing our negative beliefs and misperceptions—those blocks to new knowledge and spiritual growth that blinded and kept us from the opportunities that were available.

Spiritual law is about honoring the balance that comes from an open, honest heart. Spiritual law is about truth, forgiveness, and love for all creation; it is about peacefulness and walking in the light. So remember to honor the lessons you have learned in the past, those in the present that you create, and those in the future that you inspire. Be ready and open to change—because it is *your* creation.

As enlightened humans, we create in compassion and with power when we seek the good of all involved. Each of us is responsible for seeking guidance and following our own truth. As we seek to follow our truth, we honor those around us and naturally seek that which promotes unity and peace.

Accept Your Blessings

From your inner sacred space, you can touch your future and bring grace and blessings to your present. By going within, you create the space to see and hear things clearly, freeing yourself to choose the steps that will manifest your desires. As you continue your inner journey, relax and confidently accept the wonders and information revealed to you from within.

With Great Spirit leading us through the various levels of consciousness within our bodies, minds, spirit, and emotions, we move gently and smoothly, without alarm or discomfort. We can trust that Spirit will guide us through our shadows, doubts, and fears into the greatness of our own inner knowing. We are protected and surrounded in this awesome love as we begin to see our future and know our own path.

As you accept the growth and development of your intuitive powers, you will realize that there is no need to fake them, embellish them, or ignore them. Rather, you may find yourself becoming friends with your higher powers. Through these spiritual powers, you may enter into new realms with a heightened sense of awareness. As you enter other realms and dimensions, logic may not work; yet you will intuitively know what to do and say.

For example, have your ever noticed how time seems to slow down to permit you to complete a task or avoid an accident? Quite often, what we need to do or say will be explicitly clear within such altered states of consciousness. We may perform as though we are on automatic pilot or "in the zone."

As you more consciously accept your healing and transformative abilities, you may know greater things and even achieve greater powers. As you accept these gifts, you can also relax and enjoy the flow of love and energy coming to you, through you, and around you.

Accept Your Daily Blessings

Notice the nuances of everything you sense and feel. Pay attention and touch the Earth. Be aware of your total self, making use of logic, spirit, and mind as well as body, intuition, imagination, and emotions.

Lavishly give to all of yourself in love and joy. Take time to have some physical fun: go for a bike ride, play tennis, go snow-machining, or take a walk in the moonlight.

Indulge yourself with mental challenges, such as a game of solitaire, a crossword puzzle, or an all-night Scrabble party with friends.

Use physical exercise to keep your muscles revved up, but give yourself quiet time too, by soaking in a bubble bath, reading a good book, or taking off for a weekend spiritual retreat.

Share jokes and laughter with friends; practice the art of joyful thinking! All these—and more—are simple, wonderful ways to accept your daily blessings.

Be Alive

An attitude of self-respect attracts like-minded people, so walk tall and be proud of your accomplishments! Be attentive to the rhythms of your body and nature. Be open to the flow of universal energy that offers so many powerful gifts to you. Breathe in the joy and happiness of life. Fill yourself with the beauty and energy of nature while giving gratitude and appreciation for all this and more. Breathe deeply and fill yourself with life, excitement, and exuberance in all that you do.

Expect the unexpected. Think fast, drawing upon your keen senses and perceptions. Avoid drama in the home and workplace, and accept only those things that you enjoy doing. Use strategy, intuition, and instinct while bypassing struggle. Being alive means moving in a flash when opportunity presents itself.

By being more of ourselves, we make ourselves happy. Thus, as you feel yourself becoming more free, joyous, and alive, you will also exude the brilliance, charm, laughter, wit, and intelligence that are within. Stay focused, and know what you want. Give thanks to Great Spirit as you channel the light, love, energy, brilliance, and wisdom from within your being.

As we exude the spirit from within, we also become a beacon of light to others. We naturally bring joy, laughter, insights, wisdom, understanding, and compassion to those around us. We offer helpful suggestions and help people to help themselves, without assuming their burdens.

Present in the Moment

Did you know that even a small task can enlighten us? Next time, as you go about cleaning house, try this. Notice each picture, fixture, or book as you dust. Give thanks and loving appreciation for all that you have—each book, each table, each vase or chair. If you hire help, then give thanks and gratitude for the person who frees you to do and be other things. As you celebrate all that you are and all that you have, you become fully present and in the moment. So no matter what you do, allow yourself to be alive. Be in the moment, fully awake and aware.

I once had a vision of returning to God. In that vision, as I approached the presence of God/Goddess/Great Spirit, I lay prostrate before an all-knowing being. I saw myself as a spark of that great being. I also observed all others as sparks of that being. I felt waves of knowledge wash over me, then waves of love, until that love became absolute wisdom. I did not wish to depart that presence, but I was told that it was not yet my time. I had to return to the Earth plane, and when it was time to return here, I would quickly depart my body.

Upon returning to my physical body, I felt every cell of my being tingling as though it were a new creation, filled with life, love, energy, and power. I was radiant, alive, and vibrating with the energy of love, knowledge, and wisdom. I was filled with god-presence and unable to speak because of the awesome feelings that were sweeping through me, over me, and beyond. I was so very alive and one with God, the universe, and all of life on Earth.

Being alive is being fully present to your god-self in your physical, mental, emotional, and spiritual being. To be alive is to be totally at one with all of life, open to all of what life offers.

Open to Possibility

As you let old habits effortlessly fall away, you may begin to recognize a vision of your future. You may even realize that you have been gazing on it for a very long time. Perhaps this dream once seemed beyond your reach, or too subtle to recognize until now. Perhaps you even thought it was not a part of you. As you continue to grow and evolve, however, you may recognize the vision as one possibility of your future.

As you have been learning to balance your energy in body, mind, spirit, and emotions by being totally honest with yourself and your life, you come to know more clearly in your heart what you must do. You must also have the courage to do it.

We all must express our beliefs and follow our hearts. The challenges may be numerous, but the rewards are abundantly gratifying. So keep the peace as you proceed, but focus on your truth. When it is necessary to express your deeper beliefs to others, be gentle and take care to couch your words in kindness. Remember, just because you know your own truth doesn't mean you have to clobber others with theirs. So practice compassion and look for the good of all in actions and words.

How Open is Open?

As we address others, it may be wise to check our boundaries in order to protect ourselves and invite in only that which we desire—that is, only those experiences that we are prepared to handle.

You know what you can handle, because you have been practicing courage and acting with courage. You may also realize, however, that what makes you stronger is dealing with your own issues and not those of others.

As you proceed, therefore, you might create a personal shield of energy by calling on your guides to protect you, to surround you with white light and an impenetrable mirror-like substance.

As you become aware of all that is negative about you, you can further transform those energies and continue to define your personal sense of space. Thus, always carefully observe what is in your space. Did you invite it in? Is this your dream or someone else's? It is important to honor your desires for fun, excitement, and happiness in your space, but be honest with yourself too.

Each time we dare to be who we really are, we become stronger. Our awareness becomes sharper and clearer, and we may create bridges and connections to achieve more than we previously thought we could.

Like a planetary shift, a new vista opens for us to see into the future. It's as if a veil is lifted and now we can see forever with understanding, wisdom, and love. The intricacies of our inner lives and dreams are illuminated, along with images of our future selves. It is a new beginning, a new birth. We may create all and anything that we desire. This is an awesome, quiet power—vast and silent. This is the Great Void within our being, that great place of creation.

Choose Your Dream

The importance of dreaming and imagining a life you wish to live is greater than you realize. Have you ever wakened suddenly from your sleep, only to marvel at what you did in your dreams? Did you ever wish you could have the same wonder, joy, and awe of dreaming within the life you wish to live? This is exactly how your daydreams are just as important as your night dreams—and maybe even more important.

So continue to dream your future as vividly as you can. Pay attention to the symbols within your dreams and daydreams. Notice the life lessons that call to you.

Every now and again, however, we must step back and scrutinize ourselves. In order to learn from our mistakes, we often need to look at the obvious. We can do this lightly, laughing and proceeding in humor, as we observe, on all levels of consciousness, our present situation.

Just as you might sit in an airport and observe other people passing before you, it's a very helpful thing to take some time each day to watch what you are really doing, saying, thinking, feeling, and dreaming. Are your actions tainted with self-sabotage or self-deception? What have you learned and changed in your life? Do you like who you are? Be observant of yourself.

We are the dreamers. We have the power to change all situations in which we find ourselves. So pay attention to what thoughts and ideas direct your future. Are you proceeding with your hopes and dreams, or is fear running the show? Are you pursuing happiness and empowering yourself, or are you running in fear of failure—or success? Are you denying who you really are? Pay attention to all the clues and cues in your life. Breathe deeply, relax, and release what binds you. Choose to consciously enter into the flow of your own life. Choose to dream your future and live your dreams.

A Dream Come True

When I decided to go to law school, I didn't have a penny. I didn't even have a job. Yet I knew this was something that I greatly wished to pursue. As I focused on the desire of my dream, I suddenly became aware of community events that addressed educational scholarships and student loans. I went to listen to people speaking about their educational pursuits. I began to visualize myself after law school. Even during the dreary parts of my undergraduate years, I could still see the vision of where I was going.

When I lifted my focus beyond the toil and sacrifices of time, sleep, and hunger to the vision of where I was going, time flew by. I didn't have time to dwell on the hard parts. Difficulties were only temporary inconveniencies to overcome and lessons to recall during the next phase of my effort.

Then, suddenly, I was graduating from law school. As I walked up for my diploma, I recalled that early vision. I saw how it had carried me through, over, and around many obstacles. That dream carried me to its fulfillment. It was then that I released the vision in a sigh of deep gratitude, with deep appreciation for my guides and for my own accomplishment.

Proceed in Grace

Act now for personal transformation. Spread your butterfly wings and take flight. It is time for you to soar. As you listen to your spirit guides, to your body, and to Great Spirit, you honor your destiny and allow your own power to lead you, without expecting others to follow.

Focus on seeking the truth in all things. Leave any person, place, or thing that does not contribute to your well-being or to replenishing your power. Follow your heart and honor your body.

If your heart's desire is to be president of the company, go for it! Assess the situation, seek a mentor, devise a plan, and stay open to all opportunities that lead to that role. Visualize it.

Much will be demanded as your journey continues, so proceed in grace, dignity, honor, and integrity. Stay balanced, and rely on laughter and humor to keep you honest, balanced, and healthy. Pay attention to all that life presents, and be open to receiving the powers that the universe offers as a means to handle all situations.

This is the time you have been preparing for it since birth! You are blessed, and you are graced with confidence: you are ready, willing, and able to perform all tasks.

So go forth in happiness, confidence, love, delight, magnificence, wonder, and awesomeness. Your day has come. Walk in dignity in the grace and beauty of God. Humbly accept promotions and recognition. Celebrate your achievements, and thank those who helped you along the way. Stepping out into the fullness of life while pursuing your dreams, follow your heart with confidence.

Reflections on Grace

I came to understand grace most deeply as I observed and listened to my mother. She was born into poverty and orphaned as a small child. She and her siblings were separated into different families. She was the eldest, and over the years, she watched as her siblings died from various illnesses.

Perhaps the hardest letting-go was of her last sister, my Aunt Ruth. Ruth was married with five children when she died. Yet despite all the hardships in my mother's life—including the death of five of her own infants—she was the epitome of grace, love, kindness, compassion, laughter, and humor. My mother chose love, beauty, kindness, and compassion and soared over all that life had to offer.

My mother is my hero, my guide, and my role model for victory. She represents for me a depth of beauty and love, for she paved the way for me to proceed in grace, dignity, integrity, and praise.

Celebrate

Welcome your gifts as you appreciate each new day. Be adventurous and open to ever more discovery of yourself. Honor and live each moment with relish. Celebrate life with wild enthusiasm in all that you do. Play hard, work hard, and pray hard.

Using your powers of faith and trust, know that Great Spirit blesses you with ample opportunities and with the talent to overcome all obstacles. Find the way that benefits you most while simultaneously making use of your talents. What do you enjoy doing? What do you do well that you can do with ease? Trust that the doors will be open for you and that the gifts of love, joy, wealth, and companionship shall be given to you.

Retain the precious delights of imagination and creativity. Rekindle the laughter, excitement, and exuberance that you knew as a child. Give freely. Compliment others for their achievements, and invite them to play. Indeed, allow your gentle, loving nature to flow out to others. Be playful and childlike in your trust and faith. Delight in the wonders and joy of everyday living.

Spread joy, peace, and the ability to dream. Be a mentor to others in work and spiritual development. Share your wealth and time. Teach people to record and recognize their own growth and success. Show them how to find their own possibilities, how to accept and create change, and how to surrender to their intuition and inner knowing.

This is how you might teach people to break the illusions of their lives, to make desired changes, and to grow. As they open themselves ever wider to the gifts of Spirit, they too will enter Higher Realms and overcome fears and self-imposed limits. Teach others to relish and enjoy their successes and to give thanks for all that they receive.

Teach others to celebrate each moment of their lives, just as you do. Show them that celebration can be found in recognition, praise, laughter, prayer, appreciation, thanks, and gratitude. Celebration is the party of life.

Stick Dance

In my tradition, there is a ceremony called a Stick Dance. It is the spiritual release of a loved one who has been lost in death, yet it is also a celebration of their life.

We prepare for the celebration and release for about two years. During that time, we prepare clothing and gifts that we will give to those who helped us during our time of mourning.

When the time for the Stick Dance arrives, it is a weeklong celebration. There is singing and dancing, though it first begins in mourning. Then, midway through the ceremonial week, the energy of the song and dance changes to celebration and release. We focus on the wonder and goodness of the person who has passed, and we focus on the wonder, goodness, compassion, and love of those who helped us through our darkness.

There is great joy, excitement, appreciation, and gratitude for our loved one, our people, God/Goddess/Great Spirit, and for life itself. In the process, we are all renewed and energized, ready to once again take flight in the newness of the coming day.

Let Yourself Soar

Great Spirit empowers you and lifts you into Higher Realms, while keeping you connected and balanced on Mother Earth. Your quick insight and ability to soar come from all the lessons you have learned and practiced in your daily life. Now is the time to gather your courage and follow your heart. Now is the time to become an adventurous cocreator, singing and dancing a new design for your life. It truly is time for you to soar!

Stop walking in the shadows of your former selves. Move beyond that to see the beauty and grace of both light and darkness. Release sorrow, pain, and mourning. Be happy. Gift yourself daily with the freedom to follow the desires of your heart.

Know that we are all inherently good. See the beauty of your true self—that fun, loving, witty, charming, courteous, and magnificent self that is you! Know your self-worth and the awesome power you hold. Allow your exciting, vivacious, energetic-self free rein as you travel lightly upon the Earth.

Heal yourself with love. This means to love yourself as Great Spirit loves you—completely, freely, unconditionally, joyously, warmly, and tenderly. It means to love yourself as compassionately as a parent loves and cherishes a small child.

Let go. Let yourself soar. Permit yourself to be carried off by Spirit. See the vision from high above as Spirit sees your life. Soar with eagles! Fly with eagles as a prayer lifted to God, soaring in its manifestation. This is your destiny.

Soar!

As you gaze, dream and reflect on the flight of eagles, know that it is you. *You* are the one soaring. *You* are the one who reaches out to God/Goddess/Great Spirit. *You* are the one touched by God/Goddess/Great Spirit. *You* are the one loved, cherished, and called into being.

You are the love, the beauty, the wit, the charm and delight of God. God's creation, unfolding in all the magnificence and beauty designed by God. All this and more unfolds into the unique being and beauty that you are. God said, "It is good!" In that goodness, God saw *you* as the beautiful and magnificent person and being and creation that you are.

Prayer of Release and Surrender

I now release all the pain, darkness, and negative memories of my life as I accept their lessons and bring those lessons into fruition in my present. I surrender to those teachings, blessings, and experiences. I am grateful for the adventures and past-life knowledge. I release all the hurtful, unpleasant sensations, experiences, and memories to Mother Earth to be cleansed and purified. I now claim all of the love and acts of kindness, truth, and godliness from my memories.

I accept, acknowledge, and honor my own godliness and godly powers, abilities, and love. I believe, proclaim, and announce to the universe my declaration that I deserve the very best of everything. I open myself to receiving that abundance and love, those insights and visions. I will too fly with eagles as I ride the breeze of Great Spirit. I welcome my balanced, broader sense of self. I sing the song of my new self-creation in praise and glory.

I now acknowledge the longings of my heart and proclaim my single-minded desire to achieve my dreams. I surrender to the lessons of providence and commit to passing through the illusions of my life, receiving their lessons and releasing the negative. I promise to share the knowledge that I learn. I surrender my willfulness and stubbornness; I release my old habits, misperceptions, assumptions, and beliefs. I offer my will, myself, my all, my life back to God for my own good. God's will empowers me to act for my own good. I trust myself to live with courage and to receive love, abundance, and happiness as I pursue my life in a conscious manner.

I praise you, Great Spirit, because I am free to ride your breeze. I offer thanksgiving and praise because I have awakened to your awesomeness in my life. I offer you my body, mind, spirit, and emotions in humility and exaltation as I enter your light and love. With happiness and joy, gratitude and appreciation, I soar with your eagles in praise and in the prayer that is my life. And so it is.

978-0-595-40114-7
0-595-40114-7

Printed in the United States
62841LVS00005B/304-321

9 780595 401147